◉ INDEX

4   **AN INFORMATIONAL RIGHT TO THE CITY?**
Joe Shaw and Mark Graham
University of Oxford

6   **ACCESS DENIED: SNAPSHOTS OF EXCLUSION AND ENFORCEMENT IN THE SMART CITY**
Jathan Sadowski
Arizona State University

12   **THE JERUSALEMS ON THE MAP**
Valentina Carraro and Bart Wissink
City University of Hong Kong

16   **RENT, DATAFICATION, AND THE AUTOMATED LANDLORD**
Desiree Fields
University of Sheffield

20   **DIGITAL LABOURERS OF THE CITY, UNITE!**
Kurt Iveson
University of Sydney

24   **RE-POLITICIZING DATA**
Taylor Shelton
University of Kentucky

28   **THE #DIGITALLIBERTIES CROSS-PARTY CAMPAIGN**
Sophia Drakopoulou
Middlesex University

30   **THE CITY IS OURS (IF WE DECIDE IT IS)**
Mark Purcell
University of Washington

AN INFORMATIONAL RIGHT TO THE CITY?

Joe Shaw and Mark Graham
University of Oxford (joe.shaw@oii.ox.ac.uk / mark.graham@oii.ox.ac.uk)

Digital technologies and the people, machines, and information they connect, have redefined urban life in the twenty-first century. Everyday life is enmeshed by it. Throughout work, leisure, consumption and production; almost every thing and every place is now mirrored, represented, mediated, or shared online as digital. Even for those that profess to reject such technologies, their surrounding city's social, economic and material reality is now unavoidably dependent upon electronic flows of bits and bytes. Applications redirect individuals based on secret pathfinding algorithms; review sites tell us which are the best and worst neighbourhoods; city governments and insurance agencies have taken their operations to social media; city governance is ever more reliant on 'smart' sensors and feedback mechanisms. Cities have become more than bricks and mortar: they are their digital presences, and they are constantly performed and reproduced as such.

Digital representations are but one example of how this situation can affect us all: when you type the word "Jerusalem" into Google you are shown an infobox declaring the city to be the "Capital of Israel" (at the time of publication). No matter your own view on this, it is contested: the State of Israel is the only country on Earth to recognise the city as Israel's capital. Many Palestinians consider the city to be the capital of the Palestinian State. Much of the rest of the world either explicitly states that the city isn't a capital, or refuses to take a position on the issue.

Despite Google's claimed objectivity, this is but one example of the way in which not all places are seen the same, and not all people see the same place. Borders are displayed differently within the search engine depending upon which country the user views them from; businesses engage in 'radius bidding' to subtly alert users with the right profile to a different service provider; entire neighbourhoods appear devoid of activity, and risk becoming the informational ghettos of the twenty-first century.[1]

A lot of people interact with or consume this information. Google currently mediates over 90-95% of search requests in Europe and the USA. We believe that this dominant abstract presence has the power to reproduce and change our material reality. If you accept this premise, then we need to ask important questions about what rights citizens

---

1 *Shaw, J., and Graham, M. (2017) An Informational Right to the City? Antipode.*

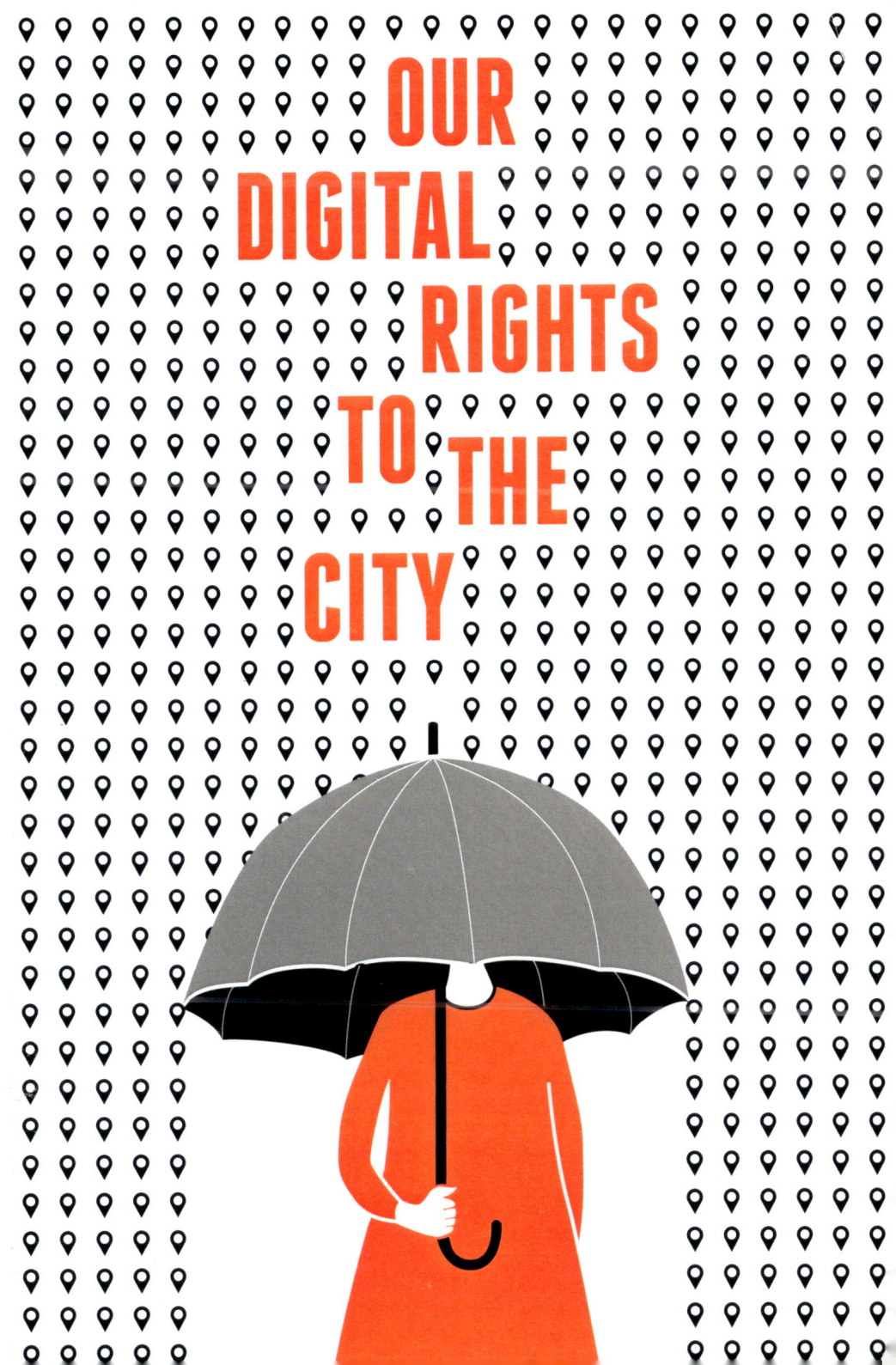

Edited by **Joe Shaw & Mark Graham**
Design by **www.irenebeltrame.com**

Published by **Meatspace Press** 2017
Creative Commons BY-NC-SA License.
ISBN 978-0-9955776-0-2

have to not just public and private spaces, but also their digital equivalents. How do we disagree with these representations? How do we feel about an advertising agency like Google "organising the world's information"? If we aren't happy, then what are the alternatives?

In 1968, long before our digitally-augmented cities were ever enabled by the likes of Google, the French philosopher Henri Lefebvre outlined what he referred to as a 'right to the city.' He believed that the great potential of urban life should be open to everyone, not just the powerful elites and large corporations that own and control so much of our cities. This emphasis on reclaiming a more egalitarian and inclusive city was aimed at the traditional mediators and drivers of urban politics and inequality – landlords, the state and the police.

Whilst the 'right to the city' was never intended to be pre-defined as a list of codified laws, its embodiment as a demand or a slogan against exclusion has resulted in all sorts of shared benefits for urban citizens around the world. It has been used to frame struggles for access to clean water in South America, to sanitation in India, for new rent control laws in Berlin, and for battles for displacement compensation in South Africa. It doesn't always work, but in the right hands it can serve as a powerful conceptual weapon for the collective good – it can represent the right to change ourselves by changing the city.

If our cities are now digital as well as material, then the struggle for more egalitarian rights to the city must move beyond a sole focus on material spaces and into the realm of the digital. In the example above, one concern might be the fact that corporate giants like Google mediate a vast amount of information about our cities. In other areas, it might be that other concerns arise, like the right to housing or to employment. The socio-economic disruption entailed by technology has often been entwined with urban development, but in the age of Uber; TripAdvisor; TaskRabbit; 'Smart Cities' and social media, all these battles have taken on new forms.

This short collection of articles explores the different way in which information technologies can reconfigure, reproduce or amplify socio-economic injustices throughout our cities – from smartphones to ID-cards, and all sorts of applications that might rent accommodation or sell labour. We, the authors, believe that everyone needs to consider these issues in order to live a prosperous city life. And we hope that this short pamphlet will help you, the reader, be more informed and able to act and interact with the digital world in a way that will help you live in the kind of city that you want.

> **We believe that this dominant abstract presence has the power to reproduce and change our material reality.**

ACCESS DENIED:
SNAPSHOTS OF EXCLUSION AND ENFORCEMENT IN THE SMART CITY

Jathan Sadowski
Delft University of Technology (J.W.Sadowski@tudelft.nl)

 "Ask my guy how he thought travelling the world sound / Found it hard to imagine he hadn't been past downtown"

Common, "Respiration"

Not long ago the apartment complex where I live decided to upgrade its security by installing gates at every entrance. Opening these gates requires a plastic fob, which works like a keycard (by pressing it against a receiver at the pedestrian gate) and like a garage door opener (by clicking a button on it for the vehicle gate). The new electronic entrances seemed unnecessary, but I thought they would just be a minor inconvenience; one more step to go through, another thing hanging on my keychain.

However, as if to demonstrate how arbitrarily they can exercise control over access to my apartment, the complex's managers did not ensure the security system worked properly before installing it. So for weeks my fob would only work part of the time, effectively locking me out of my home until a fellow resident came along and let me in from the inside. Or, if I were feeling adventurous, I could attempt to climb the concrete wall and metal gate. People began trying to prop the gate open, but the complex's workers were ordered to remove any props. It didn't matter that the control system wasn't operating the way it was intended. Its integrity had to be maintained and its commands had to be obeyed.

The other residents and I were forced to experience the exact frustration that Gilles Deleuze described in his prescient 1992 essay "Postscript on the Societies of Control": "[Imagine] a city where one would be able to leave one's apartment, one's street, one's neighborhood, thanks to one's (dividual) electronic card that raises a given barrier; but the card could just as easily be rejected on a given day or between certain hours; what counts is not the barrier but the computer that tracks each person's position—licit or illicit—and effects a universal modulation."[1] When Deleuze originally wrote this example it sounded like cyber-punk science fiction, but now it is a realistic description of modern cities.

Compared to other possible consequences of control, the electronic gates were

---

1   Deleuze, G. (1992). "Postscript on the Societies of Control." October 59 (Winter): 3-7.

only relatively inconvenient and annoying. But they illustrate the control logic that colonizes everyday life, filling it with checkpoints that regulate access and enforce exclusion. When everything matches up, when everything works smoothly and efficiently, we have no cause to pause. We hardly notice the systems that are constantly monitoring us—until they decide your "password" is invalid.

In this essay, I describe three techno-political trends that are converging in powerful ways. By following the logic of those trends I sketch two short snapshots that portray plausible near futures. I end by reflecting on features of an informational right to the city that would help derail the realization of these wicked outcomes. In short, my goal is to provide a warning about where we are heading if we do not change course.

TECHNO-POLITICAL TRENDS

1) Cities around the world are being permeated with so-called "smart" systems composed of ubiquitous sensing, data collection, real-time analytics, networked things, algorithmic processes, and central command centers. As an urban planning and governance movement, smart urbanism constructs the city as a "system of systems"—which can be rendered legible and observable, treated as knowable and understandable, subjected to regimes of surveillance and control. The aim is for people and places to be totally monitored, measured, and managed. The smart city is not just a way of bringing the convenient and cool capabilities of the smart home into the street; rather, this scaling-up involves a categorical shift in the purpose and power of these technological systems. They are fundamentally about infrastructural and civic applications. They are the kind of systems that constitute the techno-political ordering of society.[2]

2) Many powerful organizations—tech companies, finance firms, and government agencies—are, as Marion Fourcade and Kieran Healy put it, "culturally impelled by a data imperative and powerfully equipped with the tools to enact it."[3] This imperative demands the extraction of all data, from all sources, in whatever ways possible, whether there is current use for it or not. Practices of dataveillance have become so common and so varied

---

2   Sadowski, J. and Pasquale, F. (2015). "The Spectrum of Control: A Social Theory of the Smart City." *First Monday* 20(7): online
3   Fourcade, M. and Healy, K. (Forthcoming). "Seeing Like a Market." *Socio-Economic Review.* http://kieranhealy.org/files/papers/slam-2.pdf

that few people know about the systems that target them in homes, stores, streets, online, and nearly everywhere else. These systems are used to create data dossiers about each of us, they fuse and analyze data from many sources, they sort and slice us into categories, and they do so largely without our awareness and input.

3) People are subjected to innumerable scoring systems—innumerable because many of them are secretive products of guarded industries like insurance, finance, and security. These scores are created by (propriety) algorithms applied to massive databases composed of anywhere from hundreds to billions of data points about individuals and groups. Scores reduce people to single numbers that are then used to assess, judge, rank, classify, and stratify.[4] A few examples include: financial scores that regulate access to credit, employment and housing; threat scores that alert police to the danger posed by a person, address, or area; reputational scores that segment people according to their consumer behavior, social standing, economic position, and political activities. Such scores are often the outcome of opaque processes, preventing them from being challenged or changed. Despite the long list of issues related to accuracy and accountability, scoring systems continue to expand into more parts of society.

IMMINENT FUTURES

The following snapshots are based on only somewhat intensified versions of existing systems. They are not outlandish fictions, scientific or political. Nor are they meant to be like the crystal ball predictions that naïve futurists peddle. The short scenarios I portray are plausible and achievable in the very near future. The unnamed city in each snapshot is influenced by a US context. However, precursors to the technologies and policies I describe are present in cities around the world. Similar situations are emerging in

---

4   Pasquale, F. (2015). *The Black Box Society: The Secret Algorithms that Control Money and Information.* Cambridge, MA: Harvard University Press.

places from London and Rio de Janeiro to Johannesburg and Singapore.

Snapshot 1): *"We're sorry," reads the screen on the gated entry to the boutique mall, "our systems indicate that your credit score is not sufficient to enter this location. Access denied."* The gate's auto-locks engage, while notifications sent to private security forces alert them to a possible situation.

Few urban spaces are truly public anymore. Parks, monuments, neighborhoods, and shopping areas are now products of private management. They are patrolled by security forces, governed by conduct codes, and enclosed by physical barriers. The "business improvement districts" used to carve out parts of the city—and formally hand socio-political control of them to private property owners—were a step towards making cities more entrepreneurial. However, the managerial problem plaguing these landlords remains the effective regulation of access. That is now changing thanks to smart solutions. While they once had to rely on reactive tactics like harassing people who aren't welcome, they now marshal proactive technologies against people with the wrong profile. It is easier to prevent access than to kick out.

With the help of data systems and automatic enforcement, the city is filled with enclaves that impede or allow mobility. These checkpoints ensure that places can be governed with surgical precision. The credit score detectors target low-net-worth undesirables for ejection, while also identifying high-net-worth VIPs who will be given special attention and perks. Your civic profile—the calculated aggregation of all your "relevant activities," whatever that means—may ward off suspicion and (literally) open doors, or it might trigger risk protocols like proactive searches and monitoring.

People are subjected to many other scoring systems. They simultaneously expand the horizons of some while constraining the possibilities of others. The beauty of score-based auto-enforcement is that the right kinds of people no longer have to deal with the security theater—and the inconvenience and discomfort it produces—used to weed out and deter nuisances. For others, though, the presence of inhumane, non-human security technologies is bluntly apparent. But hey, if you work hard, make responsible decisions, and please the score-makers, then maybe you too can experience the joys of a city where the frictions of everyday life drop away.

Snapshot 2): *"Alert! Due to your abnormally high threat score you are not permitted to be in this zone. Exit immediately or be detained and deported."* The announcement blares from the speakers on the drone, drowning out the whir of its quadcopter blades. The drone's "sub-lethal" armaments—pepper spray balls, dye markers, mid-range tasers—are more than capable of subduing noncompliant targets.

The old ways of keeping a community safe were so crude and manpower intensive: nosy residents channeled their energy into being neighborhood watchers; cops patrolled the streets in slow-rolling cruisers; pedestrians were deemed suspicious if they fit the description of an outsider. These methods changed once cities began instituting "safety zones," which designated certain areas of the city as protected sectors that were a privilege to enter, not a right. What signaled access? Your data is the key to entry. There is no longer a need to rely on biased profiling, when each person has a data dossier— which collates countless data points and applies analytics to paint a picture of your past, present, and future.

Moreover, a vast network of surveillance systems continuously monitors, encodes, and analyzes the city at multiple layers. There is little that happens without being recorded. The ultimate goal is to break free of spatial and temporal constraints by capturing all data. With enough processing power and storage capacity, past instances and future scenarios of the city—not just a person—can be modeled and examined. In effect, one can press rewind on the city, pause it at any point, and watch it unfold over time. Or, hit fast-forward and devise models used to inform predictive policing and anticipatory planning. These technologies provide police and city managers with powerful capacities for urban governance. Rather than confronting the vagaries of a chaotic system, they can bring order to the city.

REFLECTIONS ON AN INFORMATIONAL RIGHT

By following current techno-political logics, we see how Information and Communication Technology (ICT) systems can be used to promote further stratification, overt exclusion, and automatic enforcement.[5] These snapshots should be seen as self-preventing prophecies. However, resisting the erosion of democratic ideals like equity, access, and fairness will not come easily. People must be empowered and mobilized to act against injustice and subjugation. One method of doing so arises from affirming an informational right to the city. Such a right ought to operate in multiple forms: as a slogan, as a social movement, as a political antagonism.

According to David Harvey, "The right to the city is far more than the individual liberty to access urban resources: it is a right to change ourselves by changing the city."[6] We make the city, and the city makes us. In a time when the urban environment is crisscrossed, undergirded, and overlaid with digitality, the corollary is: We make data, and data makes

---

5   L. Shay, W. Hartzog, J. Nelson, D. Larkin, and G. Conti. (2016). "Confronting Automated Law Enforcement," In Robot Law, edited by R. Calo, M. Froomkin, and I. Kerr. Northampton, Mass.: Edward Elgar
6   Harvey, D. (2008). "The Right to the City." New Left Review 53 (October): 23-40.

us. We thus have—and must claim hold of—"the right to command the whole urban process."

An informational right recognizes the critical importance of ICT in that urban process. It is a rallying call for snatching back power from the political and technical elites who reconfigure the city as a platform for corporate smartness. It is a banner that says, 'We will not allow you to extract data from people and places, only so you can then use that data to dispossess us of control over our cities, ourselves.'

An informational right is more than a request for transparency and accuracy. It does not seek to ratify systems of exclusion and enforcement. As if they would be legitimate if only we could see their mechanisms and correct our data-driven profiles. The right is a demand for antagonism, an affirmation of techno-political contestations. It is an open and ongoing dissent: against the stabilization of power through technocratic justifications; against the securitized enclosure of the city; against stratification by data-driven scores and autocratic enforcement; and against allowing the city, and thus ourselves, to be molded by elite interests.

An informational right is a declaration that the city is for all of us—and we will not tolerate techno-political arrangements that deny us that right.

THE JERUSALEMS ON THE MAP

Valentina Carraro and Bart Wissink
City University of Hong Kong (valentina.carraro@posteo.net / bartwissink@me.com)

PROLOGUE

In 1993 the Oslo Accords are signed. Soon thereafter, Edward Said critically characterises the negotiations that resulted in this agreement as an uneven confrontation between Israelis armed with 'unmatched facts, files and power' and Palestinians caught between 'disaffection and unrealistic optimism'. Palestinians need to turn geography into resistance by creating a counter-strategy, that is, a counter-map: detailed, surveyed and drawn by Palestinians, connecting Palestinians into a greater unity, with Jerusalem at its centre.

The first thing is to grasp as concretely and as exactly as possible what the facts on the ground really are, not in order to be defeated by them, but to invent ways of countering them with our won facts and institutions, and finally of asserting our national presence [1].

The Oslo Accords avoided tackling whether Jerusalem should belong to Israel or the future Palestinian state. In theory, the city is still under international control. In practice, however, Israel has full control and regards it as its 'undivided capital'. Many maps lend legitimacy to these claims.

MAPS BETWEEN SCIENCE AND POLITICS

Maps are practical tools for navigating space. What is the shortest route home? Where is Latvia, exactly? But they are not mere factual representations. The lines delimiting Latvia on a map contribute to make Latvia what it is: a state. Whether laid out on the desks of army officers or hang in classrooms, maps shape our views of the world, producing new worlds. They are always political.

While these two ways of understanding maps are at odds with one another, to some extent we embrace both. After all, as Alan MacEachren notes, when taking a plane even a postmodernist hopes the pilot will use a map that sticks to the facts. Nonetheless, Said's words remind us that maps lay uncomfortably between

---

1. Said, E.W. (1996) 'Facts, Facts, and More Facts'. *Peace And Its Discontents: Essays on Palestine in the Middle East Peace Process.* New York: Vintage, p.31.

'science' and 'politics' – disrupting the neat boundary that we draw between the two.

DIGITAL EMPIRES?

Since the emergence of modern states in the seventeenth century, maps have been associated with state-power. Cartography was a means to control, and conquer. With digital technologies, this seems to be changing. Mosaic, the first web-browser, was launched in the same year of the Oslo Accords. We have come a long way since those first, slow-loading GIFs: map interfaces, map apps, geo-tags, 360° street view services; our geographies have changed, and so their digital representations. What happens, when corporations like Google replace the state as providers and mediators of geographic information? As the introduction to this pamphlet asks, how can we contest Google's version of the map, and Google's version of the world?

COUNTER MAPS

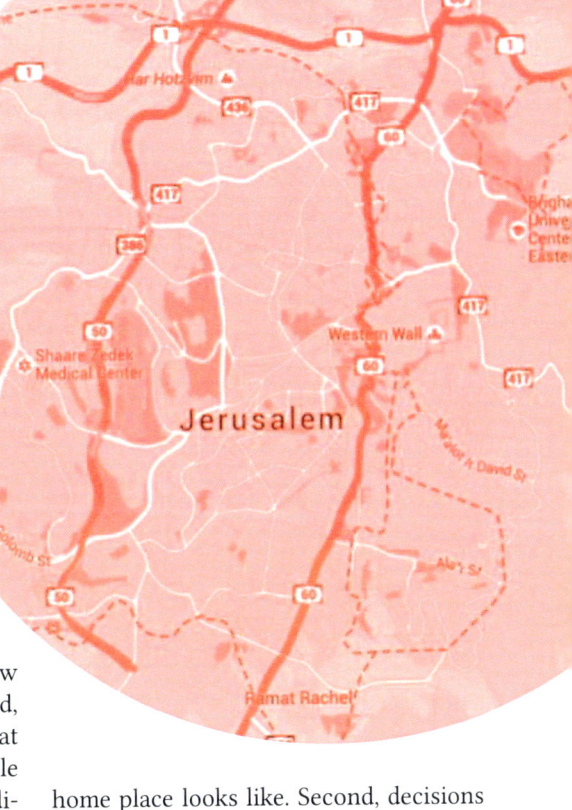

Do participatory, open-source web projects offer an alternative? Talking about maps, the most significant example of such projects is OpenStreetMap, or OSM. A Google search (we know, the irony) informs us that OSM is "a collaborative project to create a free editable map of the world". Two principles underpin OSM. First, local people should decide what the map of their home place looks like. Second, decisions about what should be mapped, and how, should be taken collectively. The result is an online mapping-project, edited thousands of times a day, by now covering nearly every corner of the planet. Maps and apps based on OSM have helped bring humanitarian aid to Haiti, improve infrastructure provision in Kenya's slums, and encourage bike-use in Austria. Appealing? Of course. But it is important to remember that OSM is not a parallel universe, where 'real world' dynamics magically disappear. OSM is part of the real world. Economic interests, ideas about gender, class and race, levels of education, geographies, geopolitics, and infrastructure: not only do they matter, but they constantly redefine what OSM is. In other words: open discussions are

13

great, but they do not guarantee everyone a fair chance to speak, nor do they necessarily result in fair outcomes.

THE JERUSALEMS ON THE MAP

This brings us back to Jerusalem, the focus of our research. As the archetypal contested city, Jerusalem is a good case study: an opportunity to look deeper into our "cartographic alternatives". The introduction to this pamphlet claims that Google improperly describes Jerusalem as the capital of Israel. However, to be precise, Google is presenting us with Wikipedia's entry about Jerusalem. So it is actually Wikipedia, a collaborative platform, that is taking a stance about geopolitics. Granted, Google plays an important role in consolidating of this 'fact'. By contrast, the map on right side of the screen sticks to the UN position, depicting the city as split along the Green Line. To the right of the line, where a majority of Israeli lives, the map is very detailed, pointing us at shops, landmarks, bus stops, etc. To the left of the line – the Palestinian half – neighbourhoods are empty grey blobs. Depending on the domain from which the map is accessed, name tags are displayed in different languages. The Arabic (and English) version of the map, however, mostly transliterates Hebrew names into Arabic, rather than adopting the names used by Palestinians. Now let us minimize that window, and bring up OSM. In case of contested spaces, OSM encourages the local community to resolve any arising dispute. The only guideline: if in doubt, what counts is what is 'on the ground'. Given that the OSM community is overwhelmingly Israeli, and that creating 'facts on the ground' is a declared Israeli strategy, both factors work at the Palestinians' disadvantage. While Google offers its map in different languages, OSM presents its data in a single map-space, where names are displayed in the 'local language'. The 'domain of Hebrew' does not stop at the armistice line, but encompasses the whole municipal administration – pushing the Israeli boundary by several kilometres.

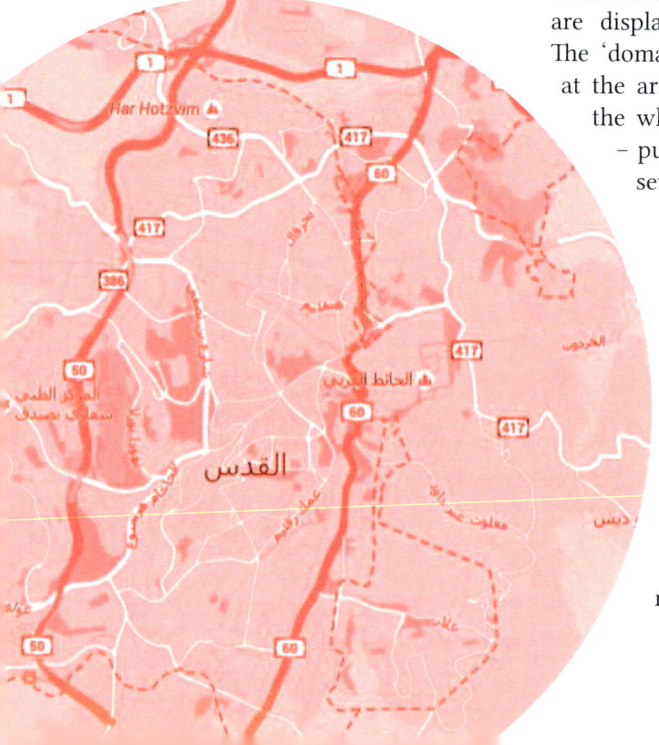

COUNTER-COUNTER MAPS

Google maps and OSM have both been used by Palestinian groups to create their own maps. In the case of Google, this has meant overlaying the standard map with new layers, showing, for example, the villages and neighbourhoods destroyed since the Nakba. By releasing its data for free reuse,

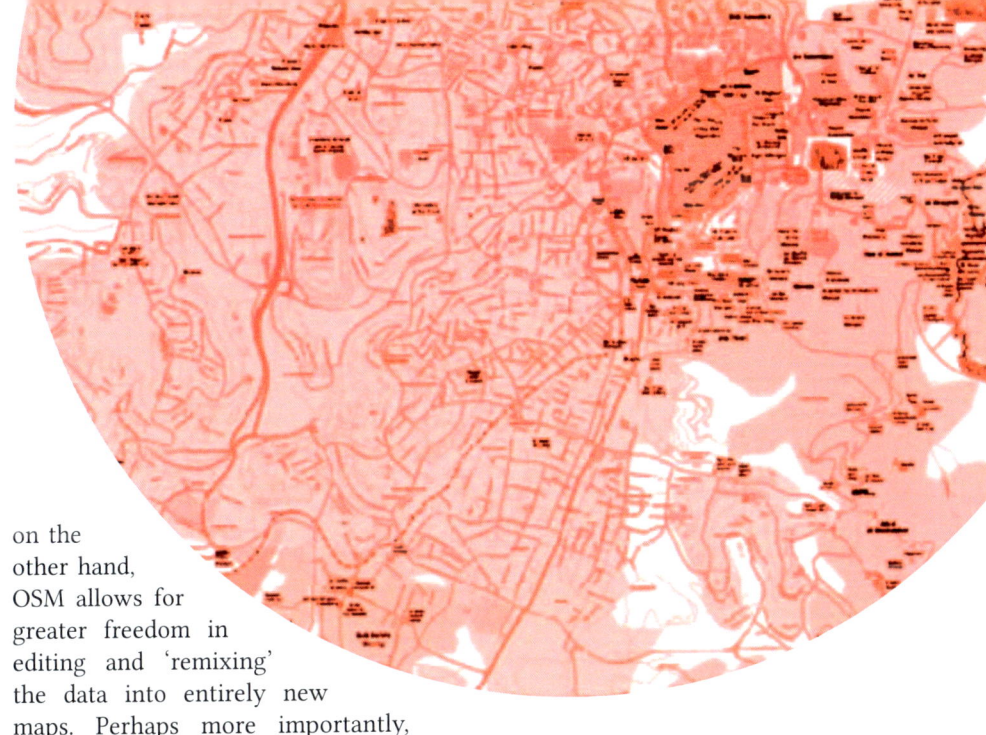

on the other hand, OSM allows for greater freedom in editing and 'remixing' the data into entirely new maps. Perhaps more importantly, OSM provides discussion forums where the community's decisions can be called into question. This is a crucial difference: not only does OSM enable groups to counter-map; it also offers a space where these different views are exchanged. Examining the debates around Jerusalem, however, shows something surprising: OSM users insist on defining this space as at once democratic and apolitical. OSM is about data, data are facts, and facts are the opposite of politics – or so goes the mantra.

EPILOGUE

Two map-applications and two models of cartographic production. But none of the resulting Jerusalems resonates with how Palestinian Jerusalemites see their city. Perhaps, a map of Jerusalem satisfying all parties involved cannot exist at this moment. Israeli and Palestinians are divided – even among themselves – about the representation of 'their' city: should it be split and how? Where are the boundaries? How should it be called? Digital technologies have made map-making easier, and multiplying the number of Jerusalems that we may find as *cartographic* representations. That said, not all maps have the same weight, so this is in itself no guarantee of fairer *political* representation. Inequalities extend to digital geographies, and influence online maps, whether provided by powerful corporations or built by a community of volunteers. This is not to say that the differences between the two models are not significant. On the contrary, to better understand what potentials and risks online maps bring with them we should look deeper into the details of maps: the fine prints in the licence agreement, the footnotes, the tags on the map feature. Maps are always political, even when rendered from open data.

RENT, DATAFICATION, AND THE AUTOMATED LANDLORD

Desiree Fields
University of Sheffield (d.fields@sheffield.ac.uk)

 "Rent Easy. Earn WaypointsTM for doing things most renters do anyway: Sign a 2 or 3 year lease. Pay rent on time. Pass tune-ups. Refer friends...Live Well. Use WaypointsTM to get these items and more for free: Free rent...Home upgrades...Appliances." *(Waypoint Homes, 2015).*

WaypointsTM are a "customized loyalty and rewards solution" designed by INCENTCO, a company drawing on technology, marketing, and industry experts to develop "incentive platforms" for real estate, furniture rental, and health care, among other businesses. For Waypoint Homes, a rental company controlling more than 30,000 formerly foreclosed homes and backed by Starwood Capital Group and Colony Capital, WaypointsTM 'gamify' the subjectivities and behaviors of 'good tenants', with renters earning points for behaviors aligned with the interests of landlords. That is, "doing things most renters do anyway" will also increase revenue per home, while many of the rewards tenants can get, such as appliances, smart home accessories and other home upgrades, also add value to the rental properties.

The US housing bust, which resulted in the repossession of millions of homes and a surge in demand for rental housing, has converged with the ascendance of the new tech boom.

Advances in (big) data generation and processing, cloud-based platforms, mobile computing, and algorithmic decision making are being used as technologies of abstraction and aggregation that allow for new forms of large-scale investment in the rental market.

Private equity firms like Blackstone, Colony Capital, and others are capitalizing on the vacant pink stucco homes, overgrown yards, and abandoned, mosquito-infested swimming pools left behind after 2008. First, they have rapidly assembled large, geographically dispersed portfolios of rental homes. Achieving this scale has then allowed them to securitize the stream of monthly payments from tenants, and these rent-backed financial instruments have met with strong demand from capital markets.

Rent payments have thus shifted: no longer the mere fulfillment of a contractual obligation between tenant and landlord, rent represents an asset base for the construction of financial products. As the example of Waypoints™ shows, information-communication technologies and data practices serve as techniques by which landlords realize rents.

In this instance, we see an incentive platform being used to encourage tenants to lock into long-term leases, which often come with rent increases, thereby securing the revenue stream to keep payments flowing to bondholders. In turn, landlords can use up-front payments from holders of rent-backed securities to finance expansion, with the new asset class also generating fees for a range of intermediaries, such as the credit rating agencies that rate the instruments and the traders that market them. Meanwhile, rewards like home upgrades flow back to the landlord in the form of enhanced property value, realized as rent at the point of resale.

At every stage of the rental process, information infrastructures and practices of data use, resue, and analysis help automate landlording. Max-bid apps allow geographically-removed investors to make local markets knowable and target the most desirable properties. Automating rent payments and maintenance requests allows for the management of portfolios of thousands of homes clustered in the US Sun Belt. Incentive platforms (like Waypoints) gamify rent extraction. Eviction can even be outsourced through software-as-a-service--already compatible with leading property management platforms.

The entrance of institutional investors into the rental market is driving the development of new applications and techniques for data generation, processing, and use to inform their investment strategies and manage their portfolios. For example, rental market intelligence (RentRange, CoreLogic), portfolio surveillance systems (Green River Capital's Rental Asset Management and Performance sys-

tem), and online marketplaces for rental investment (Roofstock, Investability) are now sites of technological innovation and expansion of the digital economy.

The role that such information infrastructures and data practices are playing in constituting the single-family rental market as a financial asset class can be seen as what information theorists like Mark Lycett, Viktor Mayer-Schonberger, and Kenneth Cukier term "datafication", or the use of data to create value. Information can be abstracted from and about specific, socio-spatially fragmented properties and tenants, and rebundled easily, efficiently, and affordably. Datafication allows for the aggregation on which the creation of new financial assets depends, and, crucially, is a self-perpetuating process, leaving new forms of data capital in its wake. For example, tenant-facing systems that automate rent-collection and maintenance requests provide a constant flow of property-level data, information that becomes data capital in the sense that firms can feed it back into their max bid algorithms, analyse rent levels, and search out efficiencies on maintenance costs.

But even as datafication makes legible previously unknown spaces and populations and informs the production of new financial asset classes, this process is often opaque to those directly affected by it, in this case renters themselves: a situation that forecloses critical reflection. The automation of so many aspects of the rental and property management process complicates the figure of the landlord: while one firm may have monopoly control over the property, a whole series of technological intermediaries is tasked with sustaining that monopoly control via systems that collect, process, and circulate information about tenants and the

spaces in which they carry out their daily lives. This raises questions about who owns that information, how it is governed, how it circulates, and to what ends it is used—and to whose benefit. Tenants of the automated landlord are effectively (and unwittingly) paying two rents: one consisting of money, the other of information, extracted as they do things like renew their lease or request a leaky faucet be fixed. Harvesting this data, in turn, creates new opportunities for capital accumulation. For example, lists of tenants that occasionally pay rent just a few days late might be sold to a data broker, and ultimately used to target ads for credit cards, payday loans, or "sharing economy" services that allow a middle class stretched thin to use their homes and cars to draw in new income streams.

Ultimately, datafication in the sphere of rental housing is working to advance the interests of financial actors by reconnecting homes into flows of global capital. At the same time, it further entangles tenants with largely unaccountable systems of information extraction and commodification. The struggle for a right to the city is unavoidably about encountering and questioning these entanglements collectively. If, as legal scholar Frank Pasquale argues, opacity and obfuscation are core to the operation of the financial and tech industries, then demystifying and making their operations visible is a political act that can open up opportunities for critique and struggle about how datafication shapes urban life.

DIGITAL LABOURERS OF THE CITY, UNITE!

Kurt Iveson
University of Sydney (kurt.iveson@sydney.edu.au)

 It may seem as though these apps are working for us – improving our experience of the city. But I think this is to put it the wrong way around – or at least, to tell only half the story. We are also working for the apps.

For growing numbers of urban inhabitants, smartphones and their mobile apps have become essential tools for everyday life.

In the decade since smartphones first became popularised, many millions of people in cities around the world have grown used to using apps for finding and making our way around the city, for hooking up with friends or potential lovers, for sharing things or thoughts or pictures, for playing games, and for many more things besides.

It may seem as though these apps are working for us – improving our experience of the city. But I think this is to put it the wrong way around – or at least, to tell only half the story. We are also working for the apps.

As use of these apps become part of our everyday movements around the city, we are performing a kind of 'digital labour' that generates vast amounts of profit for the corporations that make them. A 'right to the city' for our digitally-networked places and times will need to include an analysis of the exploitation of our digital labour, and a strategy to democratize the surplus that it generates.

URBAN LIFE AND DIGITAL LABOUR

The idea that as we use mobile apps we are performing a kind of 'digital labour' at first seems counter-intuitive. When we use these apps, aren't we just consumers of a product that someone else has made? Of course, that's part of what's going on here. But if we think about the business model of the people who own the apps, the idea that we are not just consumers but also 'digital labourers' starts to make more sense.

Many of the apps on which urban inhabitants come to depend are 'free'. But app owners are not giving us their apps out of the goodness of their hearts. The reason that their makers can give them away for little or no cost is because they (hope they) can make money in other ways. So, how do they make money?

Of course, putting up with some advertising is one of the 'costs' of using some of these apps, which depend upon advertising revenue to make some money.
But the apps that we use as we move around the city are also frequently designed to gather data about our movements. That data about our patterns of activity in the city – often referred to as a

form of 'locational' or 'geospatial' data – is a goldmine for app owners. It is sold on to third parties, who analyse that data for a variety of purposes – ranging from the provision of further commercial services to targeted advertising and security.

It's notoriously difficult to get clear information about these data markets and their value. But we can get some sense of how valuable geospatial data has become by looking at the way that markets value the apps that collect it. For instance, the real-time navigation app Waze, which works by collecting and then sharing data about its users movements across the road network, sold to Google in 2013 for a reported figure of about US$1.3 billion. That massive price is for an app that is 'free' to download and use. Those who use it to navigate the city have also been working for its owners, producing the data that allowed them to sell it at such a high price.

Waze is one of many popular mobile apps that work by enlisting us in the conscious or unconscious production of data. As we use these apps, our everyday lives outside the 'workplace' come to involve a form of labour. Such labour plays a crucial role in generating the vast market value of such apps. As digital media analyst Trebor Sholz puts it, "without being recognized as labor, our location, input, and tracked mobility become assets that can be turned into economic value."

TAKING ACTION ON DIGITAL LABOUR

If our everyday use of smart phones and their apps has become a form of digital labour, what should we do about it?

Much of the debate about our rights in the informational city has been conducted in reference to our rights as consumers. This approach tends to emphasise important issues like privacy protection and the terms of service associated with specific apps.

A digital labour perspective adds something to these discussions about our rights as consumers. It draws our attention to other issues that are crucial to the politics and political-economy of the informational city, related to our rights as producers.

As geographer David Harvey puts it, the fight for our right to the city must be a fight for "greater democratic control over the production and utilization of the surplus." If our everyday use of mobile apps produces data that is the source of massive surplus, then we have to find ways to democratise this surplus to make our cities more equitable and just.

The rights of labourers to shape the conditions of their labour and to socialise the products of their work have never been established without a struggle. And while this is a struggle for our times, perhaps there are lessons from our past to guide us.

We will need to develop new ways to assert our collective rights as labourers (alongside our individual rights as consumers). We are witnessing the birth of forms of organising on these issues. If unions offer us one historical model of how labourers have worked together to enact and protect their rights, how might we effectively adapt this model to our current situation? A few years ago, an attempt to establish a Facebook Users Union generated some media coverage, but did not catch on. What new strategies might we experiment with to collectivise as digital labourers?

We will also need to find more effective ways to collectivise and redistribute the profits that are made from our labour. Labour movements in the past have deployed good old-fashioned taxation for this purpose. Making new demands around taxation will be a challenge, but one worth pursuing given that so many of the nimble global digital corporates profiting from our labour are not paying their fair share.

"Should we feed all the data for a given problem to a computer? Why not? Because the machine only uses data based on questions that can be answered with a yes or a no. And the computer itself only responds with a yes or a no. Moreover, can anyone claim that all the data have been assembled? Who is going to legitimate this use of totality? Who is going to demonstrate that the "language of the city", to the extent that it is a language, coincides with ALGOL, Syntol, or FORTRAN, the languages of machines, and that this translation is not a betrayal? Doesn't the machine risk becoming an instrument in the hands of pressure groups and politicians? Isn't it already a weapon for those in power and those who serve them?"

Henri Lefebvre (The Urban Revolution, 1970)

RE-POLITICIZING DATA

Taylor Shelton
University of Kentucky (taylorshelton@uky.edu)

 Limiting access to property data is both an attack on citizens' right to information and an attack on their right to the city as a whole.

The dominant discourse around data today is one that tends strongly towards the post-political. That is, data is seen by everyone from government bureaucrats to Silicon Valley techno-utopians as a primary means by which political contention and disagreement is replaced with a drive towards consensus, and the erasure of claims that do not fit into such a consensus. Influenced by neoclassical economics' preoccupation with the need for perfect information, contemporary understandings of data have led to social problems being recast as information problems. The many ills facing society, and especially cities, are seen to stem from a lack of good data, which has in turn led to irrational, inefficient and suboptimal policies and decisions.

But through the increasing availability of new sources of data – whether taken from social media feeds, smartphone traces, or sensors attached to buildings, roads and water pipes – municipal governments can allegedly overcome these issues, identifying the optimal way of approaching any given problem. As the adage goes, people may be entitled to their own opinions, but they aren't entitled to their own facts.

Of course, the facts embodied in data are anything but universal. The acts of producing, analyzing and interpreting data can give rise to wildly different understandings of the world and any given phenomena within it. Decisions about what data to collect, how to collect it, how to code it, store it, analyze and interpret it, are fundamentally subjective, particular to the given individual or institution involved. Even though people might not be entitled to their own facts, this is no guarantee that the use of data will produce a single, universal answer to any given question or problem.

Nonetheless, any acknowledgment that data isn't always an appropriate solution to any given problem is largely absent from 'smart cities' initiatives being adopted around the world. Instead, urban governance is increasingly oriented towards the philosophy of "what gets measured, gets managed", finding new ways to quantify and data-fy any range of social processes. These methods are deployed by ostensibly non-ideological municipal regimes (e.g., Michael Bloomberg's New York City or Martin O'Malley's Baltimore) that are simply interested in good governance. Their view of data as always apolitical and objective provides cover for what are always intensely political and normative decisions. From privatization and cost-cutting, to union-busting and the punitive policing of marginalized communities, these data-driven policies tend to be stereotypically neoliberal.

And while these uses of data for nefarious ends help to expose the inherent politicization of such technology, many critics have failed to grasp what the geographer Elvin Wyly calls the historically contingent linkages between methodology, epistemology and politics. That is, even though data of all kinds is being used for politically reactionary means under the guise of objectivity, data itself isn't necessarily tied to these politics. Data is, has been, and can continue to be used for more liberatory purposes.

Data can not only help us to uncover previously unforeseen manifestations of unjust social practices so as to contest them, but can also be used to explicitly push back against problematic representations and understandings of urban problems such as gentrification and neighborhood change. Similarly, public policies can be contested not only through conventional political claims about who wins and who loses, but also based on the very data being used to arrive at such policy recommendations. As Greg Fischer, the mayor of Louisville, Kentucky, once opined, "Great cities embrace the data. They are not defensive about it… they improve". But if governments are to truly 'take data seriously' without getting defensive, they must take all data seriously, even if it advances an oppositional viewpoint, thus providing a point of leverage for those seeking to claim a right to the city.

Yet the ability to use data in order to create alternative representations of the city remains limited. One the one hand, the necessary skills to collect, analyze and interpret data are unevenly distributed. On the other, even for those with the requisite skills, the necessary data often remains inaccessible. Some cities around the United States have adopted open data ordinances and cumulatively opened up thousands of datasets for the purposes of promoting transparency. Yet, in an era of austerity and shrinking budgets, many municipalities are unable to devote the resources to maintaining open data repositories, making this rollout of openness uneven both topically and geographically.

This is especially true of data about one crucial facet of urban life: property. For a variety of reasons, the ability for citizens in American cities to access information about property ownership remains incredibly limited as compared with their access to data on restaurant inspections or any number of other municipal functions. While dashboards, maps and analog reports provide some access to basic information about property transactions, access to the underlying raw data remains restricted. For instance, a citizen attempting to understand speculative activity on the part of developers in a gentrifying neighborhood might be confronted in many cases not with the names of individuals or business entities with which they're familiar, but a bevy of different pseudonymous limited liability companies (LLCs): a type of incorporated business that allows proprietors to differentiate their personal assets from those of the company. Were a property-owning LLC to be sued by the municipality or by a tenant, the proprietor's personal assets would be unavailable as a potential remedy. In effect, LLCs are used to distribute liability and, at least in practice if not intent, hide the traces of predatory activity from the public. Many properties may be owned by the same individual, but with multiple LLCs each only owning a single property, making it difficult to discern any broader pattern of speculative buying. Even in those instances where someone does happen to do business under their own name, many property assessment offices require a paid account to search records by the name of the owner, rather than by a single address at a time, making it difficult to understand (and quantify) the exact scope of the problem.

In most cases, the underlying data can not only answer pressing questions about who owns property, but also about where this property is owned. This additional data-point can help to upend conventional narratives about the twin processes of neighborhood decline and gentrification being natural processes inherent to the places they take root in, and instead show them to be the result of speculative activity by outsiders – whether from wealthy enclaves elsewhere in a city, or even a different city altogether. Tying many pseudonymous LLCs back to the same owner address is a key way of identifying this kind of secretive and predatory activity. Being able to combine this ownership data and synthesize it with other data can reveal that many vacant and abandoned properties in cities might not only be owned by people who live quite far from the properties that

Absentee & non-local property ownership.
Map shows all properties in Lexington, Kentucky with registered owner addresses outside of the city. Of Lexington's 109,929 properties, 10% are owned outside of the city, representing 18% of the city's total land area.

they've let fall into disrepair, but also that these individuals and companies own dozens of other properties. In other words, this data can point towards the fundamental connection between processes of absenteeism, gentrification and neighborhood decline, as well as the mutual interdependence of rich and poor neighborhoods. Instead of seeing these places as separate and apart from one another, such maps can reveal that property ownership is one of the key means through which distinctions of rich and poor are produced in the first place. Data can help to produce understandings of urban problems that don't further stigmatize already marginalized neighborhoods, but instead situate them and their problems within a broader historical, geographical and political-economic context.

Intentionally or otherwise, limiting access to property (or any other kind of) data prevents any large-scale analysis of these processes by citizens, further disempowering them by curtailing their ability to couch their claims in the necessary language of data. Keeping such data closed isn't simply a problem because public data is paid for by citizens, or because governments should strive to be as transparent as possible. Instead, we should see limiting access to data as representing both an attack on citizens' right to information and an attack on their right to the city as a whole. In order to attain the right to both participation in, and appropriation of, the city, citizens must be free to understand the city and construct their own knowledges and representations of it; this process of knowledge production is fundamental to their ability to in turn produce an alternative, more just and liberatory future for the city itself.

THE #DIGITALLIBERTIES CROSS-PARTY CAMPAIGN

Sophia Drakopoulou
Middlesex University (s.drakopoulou@mdx.ac.uk)

The cross-party Digital Liberties campaign (#DigitalLiberties) seeks to establish a constitutional right to digital liberties in Britain.

It plans to do this either through a People's Charter of Digital Liberties or through a British Constitution that incorporates the rights of digital citizens. With a view to introducing a People's Charter of Digital Liberties in Parliament, we are crowd-sourcing public opinion on the topic. The internet is not just a commercial space; it is a community space, a learning space, and a creative space. Therefore, access to the internet should be considered as vital as access to power and water. More should be invested in infrastructure to connect remote places in the UK so that both the young and the elderly can benefit from online access.

Our actions online should not be governed by fear of surveillance. The rights of everyone, including children, should be protected online. People should own the data they create, or at least be able to gain tangible returns for the data they give away for free to companies. Irrespective of age, everyone should have the right to digital education. When I walk down a physical street I know I have certain rights as a citizen that are protected by law. The same is not true for the often-invisible, digital traces I leave behind as I walk. My phone emits its global position as it searches for Wi-Fi connections. To get to my current location, I have used my Oyster card, which tracks my transport routes around the city. My phone is logged into a social network that records my location on its system. These personal digital traces do not belong to me; in many cases, they can be used and sold by the companies that recorded them. If I use a public Wi-Fi connection, the company providing the Wi-Fi may keep my browsing history and some personal details from the device I'm using. For the sake of convenience, we trust - or assume - that we will be protected. Often, we are wrong. No law fully protects our human rights online. And that's where the problem lies. Privacy, the right to education, and freedom of speech are fundamental human rights and should apply as much online as well as offline. Around the world, there have been several attempts to address online citizenship. Brazil and Italy have introduced Bills of Rights for the Digital Citizen.

The EU has introduced directives and modified laws to protect the rights of citizens online. While these are well-intended, such as the "Cookie Directive", they are often poorly informed, full of dangerous loopholes, and obsolete by the time they are passed. Patches of laws and directives have attempted to address some aspects of our lives and actions online. But, the rights of citizens online have not been addressed in their entirety, and vital regulatory underpinnings that determine how technology can be built and deployed, such as network neutrality, data protection, and copyright are among the most-lobbied areas of legislation. The UK's referendum vote to leave the EU garding digital citizenship.

In the meantime, the internet and related technologies continue to evolve quickly, and large businesses will also see an opportunity to pursue their own agendas. The internet belongs to everyone. We should actively participate in the making of a new bill of rights that addresses our rights as citizens online. The time to act is now! If you agree with all or at least one of the assertions above, please visit our website (http://digitalliberties.org.uk), learn more about digital citizenship, use

opens a vast number of complex questions that will take many years to decide. Unknowns include whether Britain will remain within the Council of Europe and under the jurisdiction of the European Court of Human Rights (both of which are separate bodies from the EU), or create a new British constitution incorporating a new Human Rights Act. No matter how these events play out, the situation presents a great opportunity to address afresh all the grey areas of the law re- our hashtag (#DigitalLiberties), and tell us what you think! From January 2017 we will conduct a series of events all around Britain to collect people's opinions about digital citizenship and we will present these to Parliament for debate. Depending on the course of action Britain takes, we will campaign either to introduce a People's Charter of Digital Liberties or to incorporate digital citizenship rights into a new British Constitution.

THE CITY IS OURS (IF WE DECIDE IT IS)

Mark Purcell
University of Washington (mpurcell@uw.edu)

These days, a "right to the city" is often invoked among activists and reformers who hope to make the city a better place. But the term is usually understood in a liberal way, as a demand to add a right to the city to the list of individual rights that are already guaranteed by the State. But the right to the city as it was conceived in France in the 1960s, and in particular in the work of Henri Lefebvre, is a far more radical idea, one I think we should be attentive to and work to recover.

Lefebvre understood the right to the city, and the right to information as well, as part of a wider political project. That project was for people to rise up, become active, and decide to take control of their affairs in all spheres of life. This was called at the time in France *autogestion généralisée*.[1] The base term, *autogestion*, meant industrial workers taking control of their factory and managing it themselves, without owners and professional managers. The idea was not for workers to demand reforms, like a higher salary, or more rights on the job. The idea was to begin enacting a revolution. In *autogestion* workers directly appropriate the means of production and render owners and managers obsolete. *Autogestion généralisée*, for its part, was an attempt to spread autogestion beyond the working class and the factory, to all areas of life. In *autogestion généralisée*, people govern themselves instead of being governed by a State. Students and teachers govern the school instead of being governed by specialized administrators, and so on. It was in this context of *autogestion généralisée* that Lefebvre and his generation understood the right to the city. It was a declaration made by urban inhabitants that they intended to begin directly appropriating and managing the production and management of the city, instead of giving that work over to specialized experts in State agencies, public utilities, development corporations, and the like.

It is important to understand that *autogestion généralisée* was not conceived of as a utopia. The idea was not that people would take control of all spheres of their life, tomorrow, and manage them perfectly. Instead, autogestion was seen as an ongoing project whereby we declare our intention to become active and manage our affairs for ourselves, and then we set about doing so continually, resolutely, on into the future. The right to the city is precisely the same: a perpetual *project* by urban inhabitants to produce and manage urban space themselves.

If we turn our attention to the right to *information* in this context, we might be tempted to see it as a right inhabitants have to access the information they need

---

1. In English: generalized self-management.

> *The right to information signifies a declaration that we will no longer let our information be produced and managed for us, that we will produce and manage our information ourselves*

to make good decisions about the city. In that scenario, it would be a question of inhabitants struggling to gain access to existing information that is being withheld from them, by a power outside of or above them. This line of thinking would produce efforts like those of Edward Snowden or WikiLeaks. However, while such access to information is certainly important, I want to propose a deeper meaning to the right to information. In this deeper meaning, the right to information signifies a declaration that we will no longer let our information be produced and managed *for* us, that we will produce and manage our information ourselves.

There are countless examples of how we might pursue such a project, but let me sketch just a few. In its census and other data, the Indian government often underappreciates or ignores the people, activities, and human value that exists in informal settlements in Indian cities. On this basis, such settlements are often refused services, or are cleared to make way for other land uses. One response by inhabitants of informal settlements has been to carry out their own counts, surveys, and maps, so that they develop fuller information about their settlement. Not only does this work typically produce more accurate information, which is useful in getting needed services or fending off clearance and removal, but the act of producing information together is also an important means for mobilizing and activating the community. Through this activation, residents build skills, solidarity, and a sense of themselves as more capable political agents. Clearly in any such urban struggle it is important to have access to good information, but it is perhaps still more important for inhabitants to take control of the production, management, and use of that information.

A similar dynamic is discernible in the work of Los Angeles Community Action Network (LACAN). Before the new effort to put body cameras on all police officers, there was a real lack of hard evidence available to those who wanted to make a claim of police brutality, harassment, or racism. So, starting in 2005, LACAN developed a community watch program through which residents document police actions in the community, usually using video equipment, so that evidence of civil rights violations is available to those who want to file complaints.[2] As in India, the new body of information is itself an important benefit, but even more important is the activation, organization, and confidence among residents that results from having produced the information themselves.

In both cases, then, it is important to focus not only on the informational *product* but also the act of *producing* information. Urban inhabitants are not so much demanding access to some body of information that is being withheld from them, nor are they really wanting a certain body information to be produced for them. Rather, they are getting on with the job of producing, for themselves, the kind of information that they see as relevant to their project of creating the city they want.
I think we should understand both the

---

2. *This year a similar effort filmed the police shooting of Alton Sterling in Baton Rouge, LA.*

right to the city and the right to information radically, in the context of *autogestion généralisée*, as two aspects of a perpetual project through which we take up the challenge of managing our cities, our information, and our affairs ourselves.

This may seem a daunting task, one we might think we can never accomplish. But, again, *autogestion généralisée* is not a utopia; it is a perpetual project. We should not expect to *finish* it. The only thing we can do is *begin* it and continually renew our commitment to it. If we do that, I think we will discover what most of those who take up this project discover: that we are, together, better than we thought at managing our affairs for ourselves. And, what is more, we will discover that there is a great and nurturing *joy* in the project of *autogestion généralisée*. Not a cheap joy that comes and goes quickly, but an enduring joy, one that settles deep inside us and makes us stronger. A joy that nurtures us, a joy that increases our power and desire to act together. We are entirely capable of acting *for ourselves* to create the kind of city we want. And, if we decide to do so, I suspect we won't regret it. So let's get to work.

We are a group of researchers who are studying the many ways that digital technologies are rapidly changing our cities. Whilst many of these changes are sometimes exciting and unprecedented, not everyone stands to gain from them. Many people will be left behind by these transformations; many will never have a say in the types of places and societies being brought into being; and many will never actively enjoy the benefits of technologies created by others. In other words, a large number of people will be disempowered by these changes. The digital city will not be for them.

We've produced this pamphlet as an introduction to some of these concerns. We invite you to respond with questions and comments, and we hope that you can also continue this discussion.

PUBLISHED BY MEATSPACE PRESS
MEATSPACEPRESS.ORG

ISBN 0995577609